1974

Books by Hermann Hesse

Poems

Peter Camenzind

Beneath the Wheel

Gertrude

Rosshalde

Knulp

Demian

Klingsor's Last Summer

Wandering

Siddhartha

Steppenwolf

Narcissus and Goldmund

The Journey to the East

The Glass Bead Game

If the War Goes On . . .

Wandering

Wandering

Notes and Sketches by
Hermann Hesse

Translated by James Wright

Farrar, Straus & Giroux
New York

Contents

Translator's Note

My son Franz Paul worked with me on this book.
He translated the poems.
I translated the prose.
Then we helped each other.

J. W.

Farmhouse

𝕿HIS IS the house where I say goodbye. For a long time I won't see another house like this one. You see, I'm approaching a pass in the Alps, and here the northern, German architecture, and the German countryside, and the German language come to an end.

How lovely it is to cross such a boundary. The wandering man becomes a primitive man in so many ways, in the same way that the nomad is more primitive than the farmer. But the longing to get on the other side of everything already settled, this makes me, and everybody like me, a road sign to the future. If there were many other people who loathed the borders between countries as I do, then there would be no more wars and blockades. Nothing on earth is more disgusting, more contemptible than borders. They're like cannons, like generals: as long as peace, loving kindness and peace go on, nobody pays any attention to them—but as soon as war and insanity appear, they become urgent and sacred. While the war went on, how they were pain and prison to us wanderers. Devil take them!

I am making a sketch of the house in my notebook, and my eye sadly leaves the German roof, the German frame of the house, the gables, everything I love, every familiar thing.

Once again I love deeply everything at home, because I have to leave it. Tomorrow I will love other roofs, other cottages. I won't leave my heart behind me, as they say in love letters. No, I am going to carry it with me over the mountains, because I need it, always. I am a nomad, not a farmer. I am an adorer of the unfaithful, the changing, the fantastic. I don't care to secure my love to one bare place on this earth. I believe that what we love is only a symbol. Whenever our love becomes too attached to one thing, one faith, one virtue, then I become suspicious.

Good luck to the farmer! Good luck to the man who owns this place, the man who works it, the faithful, the virtuous! I can love him, I can revere him, I can envy him. But I have wasted half my life trying to live his life. I wanted to be something that I was not. I even wanted to be a poet and a middle-class person at the same time. I wanted to be an artist and a man of fantasy, but I also wanted to be a good man, a man at home. It all went on for a long time, till I knew that a man cannot be both and have both, that I am a nomad and not a farmer, a man who searches and not a man who keeps. A long time I castigated myself before gods and laws which were only idols for me. That was what I did wrong, my anguish, my complicity in the world's pain. I increased the world's guilt and anguish, by doing violence to myself, by not daring to walk toward my own salvation. The way to salvation leads neither to the left nor the right: it leads into your own heart, and there alone is God, and there alone is peace.

A damp mountain wind drifts across me, beyond me blue islands of heaven gaze down on other countries. Beneath those heavens I will be happy sometimes, and sometimes I will be homesick beneath them. The complete man that I am, the pure wanderer, mustn't think about homesickness. But I know it, I am not complete, and I do not even strive to be complete. I want to taste my homesickness, as I taste my joy.

This wind, into which I am climbing, is fragrant of beyonds and distances, of watersheds and foreign languages, of mountains and southern places. It is full of promise.

Goodbye, small farmhouse and my native country. I leave you as a young man leaves his mother: he knows it is time for him to leave her, and he knows, too, he can never leave her completely, even though he wants to.

Country Cemetery

Among crosses hung with ivy,
Gentle sunlight, fragrance, and the humming of bees.

Blessed ones, who lie sheltered,
Nestled against the heart of the good earth,

Blessed, who have come home, gentle and nameless,
To rest in the mother's lap.

But listen, from the hives and blossoms
Longing for life sings to me.

Out of the tangled roots of dreams
The long dead being breaks into the light,

The ruins of life, darkly buried,
Transform themselves and demand the present,

And the queenly earth-mother
Shudders in the effort of birth.

The sweet treasure of peace in the hollowed grave
Rocks gently as a dream in the night.

The dream of death is only the dark smoke
Under which the fires of life are burning.

Mountain Pass

Over this brave small road, the wind blows. Tree and bush are left behind, only stone and moss grow here. Nobody has anything to look for here, nobody here owns anything, up here the farmer has neither hay nor wood. But the distance beckons, longing awakens, and through rocks and swamp, snow, they have provided this good little road, which leads to other valleys, other houses, to other languages and other men.

At the highest point in the pass, I stop. The road descends on both sides, down both sides the water flows, and everything that is side by side up here finds its way down into two different worlds. The small pool that touches my shoe runs down toward the north, its water comes at last into distant cold seas. But the small snowdrift close beside it trickles toward the south, its water falls toward the Ligurian or Adriatic coast down into the sea, whose limit is Africa. But all the waters of the world find one another again, and the Arctic seas and the Nile gather together in the moist flight of clouds. The old beautiful image makes my hour holy. Every road leads us wanderers too back home.

Yet my gaze can still choose, the north and the south still belong to my eyes. Within fifty steps, only the south will

belong to me. How secretly it breathes out of its blue valleys!
How my heart beats with it! An intimation of lakes and gardens, the fragrance of wine and almonds, drifts up to me,
ancient holy message of longing, of pilgrimages to Rome.

Out of my youth my memory rings to me like bells calling
from distant valleys: the ecstasy of my first journey to the
south, the intoxicated breathing of lavish air, the gardens beside blue lakes, and listening at evening for my distant home,
across the dwindling light of snow mountains. My first prayer
before the holy places of the ancient world! And, as in a
dream, my first glimpse of the sea foaming behind brown
rocks!

Now that delight is gone, and that longing is gone, the longing to show to everybody I love those beautiful distances, my
happiness. There is no more spring in my heart. It is summer.
The greeting of strange places sounds different to me. Its echo
is quieter in my breast. I don't throw my hat into the air. I
don't sing.

But I smile, and not only with my mouth. I smile with my
soul, with my eyes, with my whole skin, and I offer these
countrysides, whose fragrances drift up to me, different
senses than those I had before, more delicate, more silent,

more finely honed, better practiced, and more grateful.
Everything belongs to me more than ever before, it speaks to
me more richly and with hundreds of nuances. My yearning
no longer paints dreamy colors across the veiled distances, my
eyes are satisfied with what exists, because they have learned
to see. The world has become lovelier than before.

The world has become lovelier. I am alone, and I don't
suffer from my loneliness. I don't want life to be anything
other than what it is. I am ready to let myself be baked in the
sun till I am done. I am eager to ripen. I am ready to die,
ready to be born again.

The world has become lovelier.

Walk at Night

I am walking late in the dust.
Shadows of walls fall down,
And through vines I can see
Moonlight across stream and road.

Songs that I sang before come
Softly once again,
And the shadows of uncounted journeys
Cross my way.

Wind and snow and the heat of years
Echo in my steps,
Summer night and blue lightning,
Storm and travel weariness.

Brown and full of this world's abundance
I feel myself drawn
Once more,
Until my path turns into the dark.

Small Town

The first small town on the southern side of the mountains. Here the true life of wandering begins, the life I love, wandering without any special direction, taking it easy in sunlight, the life of a vagabond wholly free. I am much inclined to live from my rucksack, and let my trousers fray as they like.

While I was having a drink of wine in a garden, I suddenly remembered something Ferruccio Busoni once said to me. "You look so rustic," that dear man said to me with a touch of irony the last time we saw each other—in Zurich, not so long ago. Andrea had directed a Mahler concert, we sat together in our usual restaurant, I was delighted once again at Busoni's bright pale spiritual face, at the alertness of the most glittering enemy of philistines we still have with us. —Why does this memory come back?

I know! It's not Busoni I remember, or Zurich, or Mahler. They are just the usual tricks of memory when it comes to uncomfortable things; then harmless images thrust too easily into the front of the mind. I know now! With us in that restaurant sat a blond girl, shining, her cheeks glowing, and I never said a word to her. Angel! All I had to do was look at

you, and it was suffering, it was all my delight, oh how I loved
you for that whole hour! I was eighteen years old again.

Suddenly everything is clear. Beautiful, brilliantly blond,
happy woman! I don't even remember your name. For a whole
hour I was in love with you, and today, on the sunny street in
this mountain town, I love you again for a whole hour. No
matter who has ever loved you, he never loved you more than
I do, no man ever granted you more power over himself, un-
qualified power. But I'm condemned to be untrue. I belong to
those windy voices, who don't love women, who love only
love.

All of us wanderers are made like this. A good part of our
wandering and homelessness is love, eroticism. The romanti-
cism of wandering, at least half of it, is nothing else but a
kind of eagerness for adventure. But the other half is another
eagerness—an unconscious drive to transfigure and dissolve
the erotic. We wanderers are very cunning—we develop
those feelings which are impossible to fulfill; and the love
which actually should belong to a woman, we lightly scatter
among small towns and mountains, lakes and valleys, children by the side of the road, beggars on the bridge, cows in

the pasture, birds and butterflies. We separate love from its object, love alone is enough for us, in the same way that, in wandering, we don't look for a goal, we only look for the happiness of wandering, only the wandering.

Young woman, fresh face, I don't want to know your name. I don't want to cherish and fatten my love for you. You aren't the end of my love, but its awakening, its beginning. I give this love away, to the flowers along the path, to the glitter of sunlight in my wine glass, to the red onion of the church tower. You make it possible for me to love the world.

Ah, what silly chatter! Last night in my mountain hut I dreamed about that blond girl. I was out of my mind in love with her, and would have given up all I have left of life, together with the joys of wandering, only to have her beside me. I have been thinking about her all day today. For her sake I drink my wine and eat my bread. For her sake, in my little book I make my sketches of the small town and the church tower. For her sake, I thank God—she is alive, and I got my chance to see her. For her sake, I'm going to write a song, and then get drunk on this red wine.

And sure enough: my first peace of heart in the serene

south belongs to my yearning for a luminously blond woman on the other side of the mountains. How beautiful, her fresh mouth! How beautiful, how silly, how magical—this poor life.

Lost

Sleepwalker, I feel my way through forest and gorge,
Fantastically around me a magic circle glows;
Not caring whether I'm courted or cursed,
I follow truly my inner calling.

How often that reality in which they live
Has wakened me and summoned me to itself!
I stood there disillusioned and frightened
And soon crept away again.

Oh, warm home that they steal me away from,
Oh, dream of love that they trouble in me,
I flee back to you down a thousand
Close paths, as water returns to the sea.

Springs lead me in secret with their melodies,
Dream birds ruffle their brilliant plumage;
My childhood rings forth as if it were new,
In golden strands of light and the sweet song of bees,
There I find myself sobbing near the mother again.

The Bridge

𝕿HE ROAD leads across a bridge over a mountain stream and past a waterfall. One time I walked across this stream— many times, as a matter of fact, but one walk was very special. The war was still going on, and my leave was just over, and I had to get moving again, had to hurry on country roads and railroads, to return to my duties in good time. War and responsibility, leaving and having to go back, those red certificates and green certificates, excellencies, ministers, generals, bureaucratic offices—what an improbable and shadowy world it was, and yet it went on living, it was still strong enough to poison the land, it had trumpets that could summon forth this small myself, a wanderer and painter of watercolors, it could blast me out of my refuge. The meadow lay there, and the vineyard, and beneath the bridge—it was evening—the stream wept in the darkness, and the damp reeds shivered, and the diminishing sky of evening spread out, a rose growing cold; soon the time for fireflies began. Not a stone here that I did not love. Not a drop of water in the waterfall that I wasn't grateful for, that didn't come falling from the secret chambers of God. But this was all nothing, my love for the sagging, wet bushes was just sentimental, and reality was something else, it was the war, and it rang through the general's mouth, the sergeant's mouth, and I had to run, and out of all the valleys of the world thousands of others had to run with me, and a great time had dawned. And we poor obedient beasts ran as fast as we could, and the time became even greater. But on the whole journey, the stream beneath the bridge sang in me, and echoed the gentle exhaustion of the evening heaven, and everything was altogether crazy and unhappy.

Now we are walking again, each one of us walking beside his own stream and down his own street, and we see the same old world, bushes and sloping meadows, we see them with eyes grown quieter and wearier. We think about friends who are buried, and all we know is that it had to be, and we bear it, our own sorrow.

But the lovely water, white and blue, goes on flowing down from the brown mountain, and it sings the old song, and the bushes still sit full of blackbirds. No trumpets shriek at us from the distances, and the great time consists once more of days and nights that are full of magic, and mornings and evenings, noons and twilights, and the patient heart of the world goes on beating. When we lie down in the meadow, an ear pressed to the earth, or lean out from the bridge over the water, or gaze long and long into the brilliant sky, this is our way of listening to it, the huge serene heart, and it is the heart of the mother, whose children we are.

Today, if I think about that evening when I departed from this place, I hear grief across a distance whose blueness and fragrance know nothing of battles and screams.

And some day there will be nothing left of everything that has twisted my life and grieved it and filled me so often with such anguish. Some day, with the last exhaustion, peace will come and the motherly earth will gather me back home. It won't be the end of things, only a way of being born again, a bathing and a slumber where the old and the withered sink down, where the young and new begin to breathe.

Then, with other thoughts, I will walk along streets like these, and listen to streams, and overhear what the sky says in the evening, over and over and over.

Glorious World

I feel it again and again, no matter
Whether I am old or young:
A mountain range in the night,
On the balcony a silent woman,
A white street in the moonlight curving gently away
That tears my heart with longing out of my body.

Oh burning world, oh white woman on the balcony,
Baying dog in the valley, train rolling far away,
What liars you were, how bitterly you deceived me,
Yet you turn out to be my sweetest dream and illusion.

Often I tried the frightening way of "reality,"
Where things that count are profession, law, fashion, finance,
But disillusioned and freed I fled away alone
To the other side, the place of dreams and blessed folly.

Sultry wind in the tree at night, dark gypsy woman,
World full of foolish yearning and the poet's breath,
Glorious world I always come back to,
Where your heat lightning beckons me, where your voice
    calls!

Rectory

𝔍T MAKES me lonely and homesick to wander past this beautiful house—I want silence, peace, and a middle-class life, I long for good beds, a garden bench and the fragrance of a fine kitchen, and also for a study, tobacco, and old books. And when I was young how much I despised and mocked theology! Today I know it is a discipline graceful and magical, it has nothing to do with the trivialities of meters and measures, nothing to do with the narrow history of the world, with its incessant shooting, proclamations of victory, betrayals; theology deals tenderly with inward, beloved things, grace and salvation, angels and sacraments.

How wonderful it would be for a man like me to make his home here, to be a priest! Especially a man like me! Wouldn't I be just the right kind—walking back and forth in a fine black habit, caring tenderly, even spiritually and symbolically, for the pear trellises in the garden, soothing the dying in the villages, reading old books in Latin, giving gentle orders to the cook, and on Sundays strolling across the flagstones to the church, with a good sermon in my head?

In bad weather I would make up a good fire and now and then lean against one of the green- or bluish-tile ovens, and then sometimes take my place at the window and shake my head at the weather.

But then in good weather I would walk often in the garden, to cut and bind the vines on the trellises, or stand at the open window and look out over the mountains as they become rose and gleaming out of their gray and black. Oh, I would gaze down lovingly at every wanderer who passed my quiet house, I would follow him affectionately, wishing him well, approving because he has chosen a better way than mine, because he is really and truly a guest and pilgrim on earth, instead of playing lord and master like me.

I would be that kind of priest, maybe. But maybe I would be a different kind, killing nights in my depressing study with heavy Burgundy, scuffling with a thousand devils, or waking up, terrified, from nightmares caused by my conscience, guilty because of secret sins committed with young women who came to me for confession. Or I would lock my garden's green gate and let the sexton go on ringing the bell, and I would not give a damn about my position in the church or my position in the world, and I would lie down on a fat sofa and smoke, and just be lazy. Too lazy at night to undress and, in the morning, too lazy to get up.

To put it plainly, I wouldn't really be a priest in this house. I would only be the same inconstant, harmless wanderer, the same man I am now. I wouldn't ever really be a priest, but perhaps a slightly wild theologian, a gourmet sometimes, sometimes almost obscenely lazy, surrounded by wine bottles, obsessed with nubile girls, sometimes a poet, a mime, sometimes homesick, anxious, with pain in my poverty-stricken heart.

So it is all one to me whether I gaze at the green gate, the trellises, the lovely rectory from within or without, whether from the street I gaze longingly up to the window where the spiritual man lives, or whether I gaze enviously down from the window toward the wanderers. What does it have to do with life, whether I am a priest or a vagabond in the street? It's all one to me—except for a few deep things: I feel life trembling within me, in my tongue, on the soles of my feet, in my desire or my suffering, I want my soul to be a wandering thing, able to move back into a hundred forms, I want to dream myself into priests and wanderers, female cooks and murderers, children and animals, and, more than anything else, birds and trees; that is necessary, I want it, I need it so I can go on living, and if sometime I were to lose these possibil-

ities and be caught in so-called reality, then I would rather
die.

I leaned on the fountain and made a sketch of the rectory
with its green gate, which I really like best, and with the
steeple in the background. Possibly I've made the gate greener
than it really is, and I may have made the steeple taller than it
really is. All right. All that matters is that for a quarter of an
hour this building was my home. Some day I will think of this
rectory and grow homesick, though I just stood outside and
looked at it, though I knew no one who lived in it—it will
make me homesick as if it were really my home, one of the
places where I was a child, happy. Because here, for a quarter hour, I was a child, and I was happy.

Farm

WHEN I see this blessed countryside again, at the southern foothills of the Alps, then I always feel as if I were coming home from banishment, as if I were once again on the right side of the mountains. Here the sun shines more intimately, the mountains glow with a deeper red, here chestnuts and grapes, almonds and figs are growing, the human beings are good, civilized, and friendly, even though they are poor. And everything they fashion seems so good, so precise, and so friendly, as if it were grown by nature itself. The houses, the walls, the steps up into the vineyards, the paths, the new plantings, and the terraces—everything is neither new nor old, everything appears as if it were not merely contrived, imitated from nature, but had simply risen as fields do, and trees, and moss. The walls of vineyards, the houses and the roofs of houses, they are all made of the same brown stone, and they look like one another, they are like brothers. Nothing seems alien, hostile, or violent, everything appears warm, serene, neighborly.

Sit down anywhere you like, on a wall, a stone, a tree stump, on the grass or the earth: everywhere they surround you, a painting and a poem, everywhere the world resonates beautifully and happily around you.

This is a farm where poor farmers make their home. They have no cows, only pigs, goats, and chickens; they plant grapes, corn, fruit, and vegetables. The whole house is built of stone, even the floors and the stairs; a hewn stairway leads between two stone pillars into the courtyard. Everywhere the lake gleams blue between the growing things and the stone.

Thoughts and sorrows seem to have remained on the other side of the mountains. Between tormented men and hateful deeds, a person has to think and sorrow so much! Back there it is so difficult and so desperately important to find a reason for staying alive. How else should a person go on living? Sheer misery makes one profound. —But here there are no problems, mere existence needs no justification, thinking becomes a game. A person discovers: the world is beautiful, and life is brief. Some longings remain unsatisfied; I would like to have another pair of eyes, another lung. I stretch out my legs in the grass, and I wish they could be longer.

I wish I could be a giant, then I could lie with my head near the snows on one of the Alps, lie there among the goats, with my toes splashing below in the deep lake. So I would lie there and never get up again, between my fingers the bushes would grow, and the wild roses of the Alps in my hair, my knees would be alpine foothills, and vineyards would stand on my body, and houses, and chapels. And so for ten thousand years I lie there, and gaze into the heavens, and gaze into the lake. When I sneeze, there's a thunderstorm. When I breathe, the snow melts, and the waterfalls dance. When I die, the whole world dies. Then I journey across the world's ocean, to bring back a new sun.

Where am I going to sleep tonight? Who cares! What is the world doing? Have new gods been discovered, new laws, new freedoms? Who cares! But up here a primrose is blossoming and bearing silver fuzz on its leaves, and the light sweet wind is singing below me in the poplars, and between my eyes and heaven a dark golden bee is hovering and humming—I care about that. It is humming the song of happiness, humming the song of eternity. Its song is my history of the world.

Rain

Soft rain, summer rain
Whispers from bushes, whispers from trees.
Oh, how lovely and full of blessing
To dream and be satisfied.

I was so long in the outer brightness,
I am not used to this upheaval:
Being at home in my own soul,
Never to be led elsewhere.

I want nothing, I long for nothing,
I hum gently the sounds of childhood,
And I reach home astounded
In the warm beauty of dreams.

Heart, how torn you are,
How blessed to plow down blindly,
To think nothing, to know nothing,
Only to breathe, only to feel.

Trees

𝔉OR ME, trees have always been the most penetrating preachers. I revere them when they live in tribes and families, in forests and groves. And even more I revere them when they stand alone. They are like lonely persons. Not like hermits who have stolen away out of some weakness, but like great, solitary men, like Beethoven and Nietzsche. In their highest boughs the world rustles, their roots rest in infinity; but they do not lose themselves there, they struggle with all the force of their lives for one thing only: to fulfill themselves according to their own laws, to build up their own form, to represent themselves. Nothing is holier, nothing is more exemplary than a beautiful, strong tree. When a tree is cut down and reveals its naked death-wound to the sun, one can read its whole history in the luminous, inscribed disk of its trunk: in the rings of its years, its scars, all the struggle, all the suffering, all the sickness, all the happiness and prosperity stand truly written, the narrow years and the luxurious years, the attacks withstood, the storms endured. And every young farmboy knows that the hardest and noblest wood has the narrowest rings, that high on the mountains and in continuing danger the most indestructible, the strongest, the ideal trees grow.

Trees are sanctuaries. Whoever knows how to speak to them, whoever knows how to listen to them, can learn the truth. They do not preach learning and precepts, they preach, undeterred by particulars, the ancient law of life.

A tree says: A kernel is hidden in me, a spark, a thought, I am life from eternal life. The attempt and the risk that the eternal mother took with me is unique, unique the form and veins of my skin, unique the smallest play of leaves in my branches and the smallest scar on my bark. I was made to form and reveal the eternal in my smallest special detail.

A tree says: My strength is trust. I know nothing about my fathers, I know nothing about the thousand children that every year spring out of me. I live out the secret of my seed to the very end, and I care for nothing else. I trust that God is in me. I trust that my labor is holy. Out of this trust I live.

When we are stricken and cannot bear our lives any longer, then a tree has something to say to us: Be still! Be still! Look at me! Life is not easy, life is not difficult. Those are childish thoughts. Let God speak within you, and your thoughts will grow silent. You are anxious because your path leads away from mother and home. But every step and every day lead you back again to the mother. Home is neither here nor there. Home is within you, or home is nowhere at all.

A longing to wander tears my heart when I hear trees rustling in the wind at evening. If one listens to them silently for a long time, this longing reveals its kernel, its meaning. It is not so much a matter of escaping from one's suffering, though it may seem to be so. It is a longing for home, for a memory of the mother, for new metaphors for life. It leads home. Every path leads homeward, every step is birth, every step is death, every grave is mother.

So the tree rustles in the evening, when we stand uneasy before our own childish thoughts. Trees have long thoughts, long-breathing and restful, just as they have longer lives than ours. They are wiser than we are, as long as we do not listen to them. But when we have learned how to listen to trees, then the brevity and the quickness and the childlike hastiness of our thoughts achieve an incomparable joy. Whoever has learned how to listen to trees no longer wants to be a tree. He wants to be nothing except what he is. That is home. That is happiness.

Painter's Joy

Acres bear corn and cost money.
Meadows are surrounded by barbed wire,
Terrible need and avarice laid side by side,
Everything looks wasted and closed in.

But here in my eye another order of things
Goes on living; violet ebbs away
And the purple flows on its throne, and I sing
My innocent song.

Yellow by yellow, and yellow next to red.
Cool blue turns to the color of rose.
Light and color leap from world to world,
Arch and echo away in a surging of love.

The spirit reigns, healing all sickness,
Green sings out from newborn springs,
The world will share in freshness and meaning,
And hearts grow glad and light.

Rainy Weather

ℑ T I S trying to rain, over the lake the gray and flabby air hangs anxiously. I am walking on the beach, near the inn where I am staying.

There is a kind of rainy weather that is refreshing and cheerful. Today's weather is not. The dampness falls and rises endlessly in the dense air. The clouds constantly fall apart, and new ones are always there. Irresolution and a bad mood prevail in the sky.

I thought this evening was going to be much more pleasant for me, dinner and a night's lodging at the fisherman's inn, a walk on the beach, bathing in the lake, perhaps a swim in the moonlight. Instead of these, a morbid and dark sky nervously and ill-humoredly releases its morose shower of rain into the lake, and I creep along, no less nervous and ill-humored, through the changed landscape. Perhaps I drank too much wine last evening, or too little, or else I dreamed about troubling things. God knows what it is. The mood is devilish, the air is flabby and tormenting, my thoughts are gloomy, and there is not a gleam in the world.

Tonight I will have baked fish, and drink a good deal of the local red wine. We will soon bring something gleaming back into the world, and find life more bearable. We'll have a fire in the tavern fireplace, so I won't any longer have to see or bear this lazy, slack rain. I will be smoking good long Brissago cigars and holding my wine glass up to the fire, till it glitters like a blood-colored gem. We will make it all right. The evening will go past, I will be able to sleep, tomorrow everything will be different.

In the shallow water along the beach, raindrops are splashing; a cool and moist wind fusses in the damp trees, which glow leadenly like dead fish. The devil has spit in the soup. Nothing comes out even. Nothing sounds right. Nothing rejoices and warms. Everything is desolate, sad, foul. All strings out of tune. All colors faded.

I know why this is so. It is not the wine I drank yesterday, and it is not the bad bed I slept in, and it is not even the rainy weather. Devils have been here and shrilly untuned me, string by string. The anxiety was there again, anxiety from childhood dreams, from fairy tales, from the things a schoolboy had to go through. The anxiety, the being trapped by the unalterable, the melancholy, the aversion. How insipid the world tastes! How dreadful that one has to rise again tomorrow, to eat again, to live again! Then why does one go on living? Why are we so idiotically good-natured? Why didn't we jump in the lake a long time ago?

There is no escape. You can't be a vagabond and an artist and still be a solid citizen, a wholesome, upstanding man. You want to get drunk, so you have to accept the hangover. You say yes to the sunlight and your pure fantasies, so you have to say yes to the filth and the nausea. Everything is within you, gold and mud, happiness and pain, the laughter of childhood and the apprehension of death. Say yes to everything, shirk nothing, don't try to lie to yourself. You are not a solid citizen, you are not a Greek, you are not harmonious, or the master of yourself, you are a bird in the storm. Let it storm! Let it drive you! How much you have lied! A thousand times, even in your poems and books, you have played the harmonious man, the wise man, the happy, the enlightened man. In the same way, men attacking in war have played heroes, while their bowels twitched. My God, what a poor ape, what a fencer in the mirror, man is—particularly the artist—particularly the poet—particularly myself!

I will have baked fish, and I will drink Nostrano out of a thick glass, and draw slowly on long cigars, and spit into the glowing fireplace, think about my mother, and try to press a few drops of sweetness out of my anxiety and sorrow. Then I will lie down in the inadequate bed beside the thin wall, listen to wind and rain, struggle with the beating of my heart, wish for death, fear death, call out to God. Until it is all over, until doubt wears itself out, until something like sleep and consolation beckons to me. So it was when I was twenty years old, so it is today, and so it will go on, until it ends. Always, over and over, I will have to pay for my loved and lovely life with days like these. Always, over and over, these days and nights will come, the anxiety, the aversion, the doubt. And I will still live, and I will still love life.

Oh, how meanly and maliciously the clouds hang on the mountains! How false and tinny is the flat light mirrored in the lake! How stupid and comfortless everything is, everything that comes into my mind.

Chapel

𝕿HE ROSE-RED chapel, with its small roof sloping forward, must have been built by good men of delicate feeling, and very pious men.

I hear it said so often that today there are no pious men any longer. One could just as easily say that today there is no longer any music and no longer any blue sky. I believe that many pious men exist. I am pious myself. But I wasn't always.

The way to piety may be different for different people. For me it ran through many errors and griefs, through much self-torment, through considerable stupidities, primeval forests of stupidities. I was a free spirit, and knew that piety was a sickness of the soul. I was an ascetic, and drove nails into my flesh. I did not know that piety signifies health and serenity.

To be pious is nothing else than to be trustful. Trust belongs to the simple, healthy, harmless man, the child, the wild creature. Those of us who were not simple or harmless had to find trust by roundabout ways. Trust in yourself is the beginning. Neither by retribution, nor by guilt and a bad conscience, nor by mortification and sacrifice will belief be won. All these efforts have to do with gods who dwell outside of us.

The god in which we must believe is within ourselves. Whoever says no to himself cannot say yes to God.

Oh, beloved, intimate chapels of this country! You bear the signs and inscriptions of a god who is not mine. Your believers utter prayers whose words I do not know. And yet I can still pray in you just as well as in the oak forest or in the mountain meadow. Yellow or white or color of rose, you blossom forth out of the green, like the spring songs of young men. To you, every prayer is acceptable and holy.

Prayer is as holy, as sanctifying as song. Prayer is trust, is confirmation. Whoever prays truly does not ask for anything, he merely recounts his condition and his wants, he sings forth his suffering and his thanks, as little children sing. So the blessed hermits prayed in their oasis among the deer, as they were painted in the churchyard of Pisa—that loveliest picture in the world. So trees also pray, and animals. In the pictures of a good painter, every tree and every mountain prays.

Anyone who comes from a pious Protestant home has a long way to seek before he finds prayer like this. He knows the hells of conscience, he knows the death sting of personal disintegration, he has learned division, torment, despair of every kind. Later along the path, he is astonished to see how simple, childlike, and natural blessedness is, which he had sought on such thorny ways. But the thorn-covered paths were not without value. The returned traveler is different from the man who remained at home. He loves more intimately, and he is freer from the demands of justice and delusion. Justice is the virtue of those who remain at home, an old virtue, a virtue of primitive men. We younger ones have no use for it. We know only one happiness: love; and only one virtue: trust.

As for you chapels, I envy you your believers, your members. Hundreds of worshippers pour out their suffering to you, hundreds of children tie wreaths to your doors and bring their candles to you. But our belief, the piety of those who have traveled so far, is a lonely one. Those of the old belief will not be our companions, and the currents of the world flow past far from our islands.

I pluck flowers in the nearest meadow—primrose, clover, and columbine—and lay them in the chapel. I sit down on the parapet under the sloping roof and hum my pious song in the morning stillness. My hat lies on the brown wall, and a blue butterfly comes to rest on it. In the valley far off, a train whistles thinly and gently. On the shrubbery, here and there, the morning dew is still shining.

Things Pass

From the tree of life,
Leaf after leaf falls around me.
Oh, world delighted with ecstasy,
How you fill me at last,
How you fill me with weariness,
And make me drunk!
Whatever still glows today
Is soon lost.
Soon the wind rattles
Across my withered grave,
Over the small child
The mother bends down.
Her eyes are what I want to see,
Her gaze is my star,
Everything else can appear and vanish,
Everything die, everything, good riddance.
Only the eternal mother remains,
We came from her,
And her finger writes our names
Delighted on the fleeting air.

Noon Rest

Again the sky laughs brightly, the air dances and flows over everything. The far-off strange country belongs to me again, the alien has become home. A place by a tree above the lake is mine today; I have made a sketch of a cottage with cows and clouds. I have written a letter, which I will not send. Now I unpack my lunch bag: bread, sausage, nuts, chocolate.

Nearby there is a birch wood where I saw the ground covered with dead branches. I feel like building a small fire, to take it as a companion and sit beside it. I walk over, gather a good armload of wood, lay paper underneath, and light it. The thin smoke rises up easily and happily, the bright red flame flickers strangely in the midday sunlight.

The sausage is good, tomorrow I'll buy another of the same kind. God, I wish I had a few chestnuts to roast!

After lunchtime I spread my coat on the grass, rest my head on it, and watch as my little smoke offering rises up into the bright heavens. Some music and celebration belong here. I think about songs by Eichendorff that I know by heart. Not many of them occur to me, and even then I can't recall some of the verses. I say the songs over, half singing to the melodies of Hugo Wolf and Othmar Schoeck. "Whoever longs to wander in strange lands" and "O beloved, faithful lute" are the loveliest. The songs are full of sadness, but the sadness is only a summer cloud, behind it stand trust and the sun. That is Eichendorff. In songs like these he stands above Mörike and Lenau.

If my mother were still alive now, I would think about her and try to tell her everything, to confess what she ought to know about me.

Instead, a little girl with black hair, about ten years old, comes walking past, surveys me and my small fire, accepts a nut and a piece of chocolate from me, sits beside me in the grass, and now starts telling me about her goat and about her big brother, speaking with the dignity and gravity that children have. What clowns we older persons are! Then she has to go home, she has brought lunch out to her father. She makes her farewell courteously and seriously and walks away in her wooden sandals and woolen stockings. She is called Annunziata.

The fire has gone out. The sun has gone down ever so slightly. I still want to walk a good distance today. As I begin packing and wrapping up my bundle, I think of another bit of Eichendorff, and I sing it on my knees :

Soon, oh how soon the still time will come,
When I too will rest, and over me
Will rustle the lovely loneliness of trees,
And, even here, no one will know me.

I perceive for the first time that even in this beloved passage the sadness is merely the shadow of a cloud. This sadness is nothing but the gentle music of passing things, and without it, whatever is beautiful does not touch us. It is without pain. I take it with me on my journey, and I feel contented as I step briskly farther up the mountain path, the lake far below me, past a mill brook with chestnut trees and a sleeping mill wheel, into the quiet blue day.

The Wanderer Speaking to Death

You will come to me too some day,
You will not forget me.
And the torment ends,
And the fetter breaks.

Still, you seem strange and far,
Dear brother death.
You stand like a cold star
Above my trouble.

But some day you will be near
And full of flames.
Come, beloved, I am here,
Take me, I am yours.

Lake, Tree, Mountain

ⓞNCE THERE was a lake. Above the blue lake and into the blue sky towered a spring tree, green and yellow. Beyond it the sky rested quietly on the arched mountain.

A wanderer sat at the foot of the tree. Yellow petals drifted down to his shoulders. He was tired and had closed his eyes. A dream drifted down to him from the yellow tree.

The wanderer was small, he was a boy, he heard his mother singing in the garden behind the house. He saw a butterfly fluttering, yellow and fresh, a joyous yellow in the blue sky. He ran after the butterfly. He ran across the meadow, he ran across the brook, he ran to the lake. There the butterfly flew away over the bright water, and the boy flew after it, hovered brightly and easily, flew happily through the blue space. The sun shone on his wings. He flew after the yellow and flew over the lake and over the high mountain, where God stood on a cloud and sang. Around him were the angels, and one of the angels looked like the boy's mother and held a watering can over a bed of tulips so they could drink. The boy flew to the angel, and himself became an angel, and embraced his mother.

The wanderer rubbed his eyes, and closed them again. He plucked a red tulip and pinned it to his mother's breast. He

plucked a tulip and pinned it to her hair. Angels and butterflies were flying about, and all the birds and animals and fish
in the world were there, and whenever he called them by
name, they came and flew to the boy's hand and belonged to
him, they let themselves be stroked and questioned and sent
forth again.

The wanderer woke and thought about the angel. He heard
the fine leaves rippling in the tree, and heard the delicate,
silent life rising and falling in golden streams in the tree. The
mountain looked across to him, and there God stood in his
brown cloak, singing. One could hear his song across the
glassy spaces of the lake. It was a simple song, it mingled and
sounded together with the gentle flowing of strength in the
tree, and with the gentle flowing of blood in the heart, and
with the gentle streams that came from the dream and ran
through him.

Then he himself started to sing, slowly and lingeringly. His
song was artless, it was like air and the beating of waves, it
was only a humming and buzzing like that of a bee. The song
gave answer to the singing God in the distance, and to the
singing stream in the tree, and to the running song in the
blood.

For a long time the wanderer sang, like a bluebell ringing in the spring wind and like a locust making music in the grass. He sang for as long as an hour, or a year. He sang like a child and like a god, he sang butterfly and sang mother, he sang tulip and sang lake, he sang his blood and the blood in the tree.

As he walked onward and passed without thinking into the warm countryside, his right path and his destination and his own name gradually occurred to him once more, and he recalled that it was Tuesday, and that over there the train ran toward Milan. And yet he still heard singing in the distance, coming across the lake. There God stood in his brown cloak and kept on singing, but little by little the wanderer lost the song.

Magic of Colors

God's breath, here and there,
Heaven above, heaven below,
Light sings its songs a thousand times,
God becomes the world in so many colors.

White to black, warm to cool
Feel themselves newly drawn,
And forever out of the whirling chaos
The rainbow rises.

And so God's light
Wanders in a thousand forms,
Created and shaped together.
And we cherish Him as the sun.

Clouded Sky

Dwarf shrubs blossom between the rocks. I lie and gaze into the evening sky, which for hours has been slowly covering itself with small, silent, tangled clouds. Winds must be blowing up there, though here one can't perceive a trace of them. They weave the cloud threads like yarn.

As the rising of moisture and the raining down of water on the earth follow each other in a certain rhythm, as the seasons, and ebb tide and flood tide, have fixed times and sequences, so everything within us moves according to laws and rhythms. There is one Professor Fliess, who calculated certain numerical progressions in order to indicate the periodic repetition and return of vital occurrences. It sounds like the Cabala, but presumably the Cabala is also knowledge. The very fact that German professors make fun of it speaks well for it.

The dark waves in my life, which I fear, come also with a certain regularity. I don't know the dates and numbers, I have never kept a continuing diary. I do not and will not know whether the numbers 23 and 27 or any other numbers have anything to do with it. I only know: from time to time there rises in my soul, without external cause, the dark wave. A shadow runs over the world, like the shadow of a cloud. Joy

sounds false, and music stale. Depression pervades everything, dying is better than living. Like an attack this melancholy comes from time to time, I don't know at what intervals,
and slowly covers my sky with clouds. It begins with an un-
rest in the heart, with a premonition of anxiety, probably with
my dreams at night. People, houses, colors, sounds that other-
wise please me become dubious and seem false. Music gives
me a headache. All my mail becomes upsetting and contains
hidden arrows. At such times, having to converse with people
is torture, and immediately leads to scenes. Because of times
like this, one does not own guns; for the same reason, one
misses them. Anger, suffering, and complaints are directed at
everything, at people, at animals, at the weather, at God, at
the paper in the book one is reading, at the material of the
very clothing one has on. But anger, impatience, complaints,
and hatred have no effect on things, and are deflected from
everything, back to myself. I am the one who deserves hatred.
I am the one who brings discord and hatred into the world.

I am resting after one such day. I know that for a while
now rest is to be expected. I know how beautiful the world is;
for the time being, it is more beautiful for me than for any

other person; colors fuse more delicately, the air flows more blissfully, the light hovers more tenderly. And I know that I must pay for this with the days when life is unbearable. There are good remedies against depression: song, piety, the drinking of wine, making music, writing poems, wandering. By these remedies I live, as the hermit lives by his prayers. Sometimes it seems to me that the scales have tipped, and that my good hours are too seldom and too few to make up for the bad ones. Then sometimes I find that, on the contrary, I have made progress, that the good hours have increased and the evil ones decreased. What I never wish, not even in the worst hours, is a middling ground between good and bad, a lukewarm, bearable center. No, rather an exaggeration of the curve—a worse torment and, because of it, the blessed moments even richer in their brilliance.

Despair fades away from me, life is pleasing again, the sky is beautiful again, wandering is meaningful again. On such days of return, I feel something of the mood of recovery: weariness without any particular sorrow, resignation without bitterness, gratitude without self-contempt. Slowly the lifeline begins to rise. I hum a line of a song again. I pick a flower again. I toy with my walking stick again. I have overcome it again. And I will have to overcome it once more, perhaps many times.

It would be wholly impossible for me to say whether this cloudy, silently disturbed, unraveled sky is mirrored in my soul or the reverse, whether or not I read the image of my own inner life in this sky. Sometimes everything is so completely uncertain! There are days when I am convinced that no man on earth can recognize certain moods of air and cloud, certain tones of color, certain fragrances and movements of moisture as finely, as exactly, and as truly as I can, with my old, nervous senses of poet and wanderer. And then again, as today, it can become doubtful to me whether I have seen, heard, and smelled anything after all, whether everything that I took to be true is not merely an image cast outward, the image of my inner life.

Red House

RED HOUSE, out of your small garden and vineyard all the southern Alps breathe to me. I have walked past you several times, and even the first time my wanderlust was sharply reminded of its opposite pole; and once again I toy with the old refrains: to have a home, a little house in a green garden, stillness everywhere, a village below me. In a little room facing east my bed would stand, my own bed; in another little room facing south, my table; and there I would hang up the small, ancient Madonna which I bought on an earlier journey, in Brescia.

Like the day between morning and evening, my life falls between my urge to travel and my homesickness. Maybe some day I will have come far enough for travel and distances to become part of my soul, so that I will have their images within me, without having to make them literally real any more. Maybe I will also find that secret home within me where there will be no more flirting with gardens and little red houses. To be at home with myself!

How different life would be! There would be a center, and out of that center all forces would reach.

But there is no center in my life; my life hovers between many poles and counterpoles. A longing for home here, a longing for wandering there. A longing for loneliness and cloister here, and an urge for love and community there. I have collected books and paintings and given them away. I have cultivated voluptuousness and vice, and renounced them for asceticism and penance. I have faithfully revered life as substance, and then realized that I could recognize and love life only as function.

But it is not my concern to change myself. Only a miracle could do that. And whoever seeks a miracle, whoever grasps at it, whoever tries to assist it, sees it fleeing away. My concern is to hover between many extreme opposites and to be ready when a miracle overtakes me. My concern is to be unsatisfied and to endure restlessness.

Red house in the green! I have already lived through you, I can't go on living through you. I have already had a home, I have built a house, measured wall and roof, laid out paths in the garden, and hung my own walls with my own pictures. Every person is driven to do the same—I am happy that I once lived this way. Many of my desires in life have been fulfilled. I wanted to be a poet, and became a poet. I wanted to have a house, and built one. I wanted to have a wife and children, and had them. I wanted to speak to people and impress them, and I did so. And every fulfillment quickly became satiety. But to be satisfied was the very thing I could not bear. Poetry became suspect to me. The house became narrow to me. No goal that I reached was a goal, every path was a detour, every rest gave birth to new longing.

Many detours I will still follow, many fulfillments will still disillusion me. One day, everything will reveal its meaning.

There, where contradictions die, is Nirvana. Within me, they still burn brightly, beloved stars of longing.

Evenings

Evenings the lovers walk
Slowly through the field,
Women let down their hair,
Businessmen count money,
Townspeople anxiously read the latest
In the evening paper,
Children clench tiny fists,
Sleeping deep and dark.
Each one with his own reality,
Following a noble duty,
Townspeople, infants, lovers—
And not me?

Yes! My evening tasks also,
To which I am a slave,
Cannot be done without by the spirit of the age,
They too have meaning.
And so I go up and down,
Dancing inside,
Humming foolish street songs,
Praise God and myself,
Drink wine and pretend

That I am a pasha,
Worry about my kidneys,
Smile, drink more,
Saying yes to my heart
(In the morning, this won't work),
Playfully spin a poem
Out of suffering gone by,
Gaze at the circling moon and stars,
Guessing their direction,
Feel myself one with them
On a journey
No matter where.